The Colonial Conquest of Africa

Other Books by Robin McKown

AMERICAN REVOLUTION: THE FRENCH ALLIES

CONGO: RIVER OF MYSTERY

GIANT OF THE ATOM: ERNEST RUTHERFORD

JANINE

LUMUMBA

PATRIOT OF THE UNDERGROUND

RAKOTO AND THE DRONGO BIRD

SEVEN FAMOUS TRIALS IN HISTORY

The Colonial Conquest of Africa

◄—A FIRST BOOK—►

By Robin McKown

Illustrated with prints, photographs, and maps

Franklin Watts, Inc.
845 Third Avenue
New York, New York 10022

Maps by George Buctel

SBN 531-00743-X
Copyright © 1971 by Franklin Watts, Inc.
Library of Congress Catalog Card Number: 71–158424
Printed in the United States of America

1 2 3 4 5

Contents

The Colonial Conquest of Africa

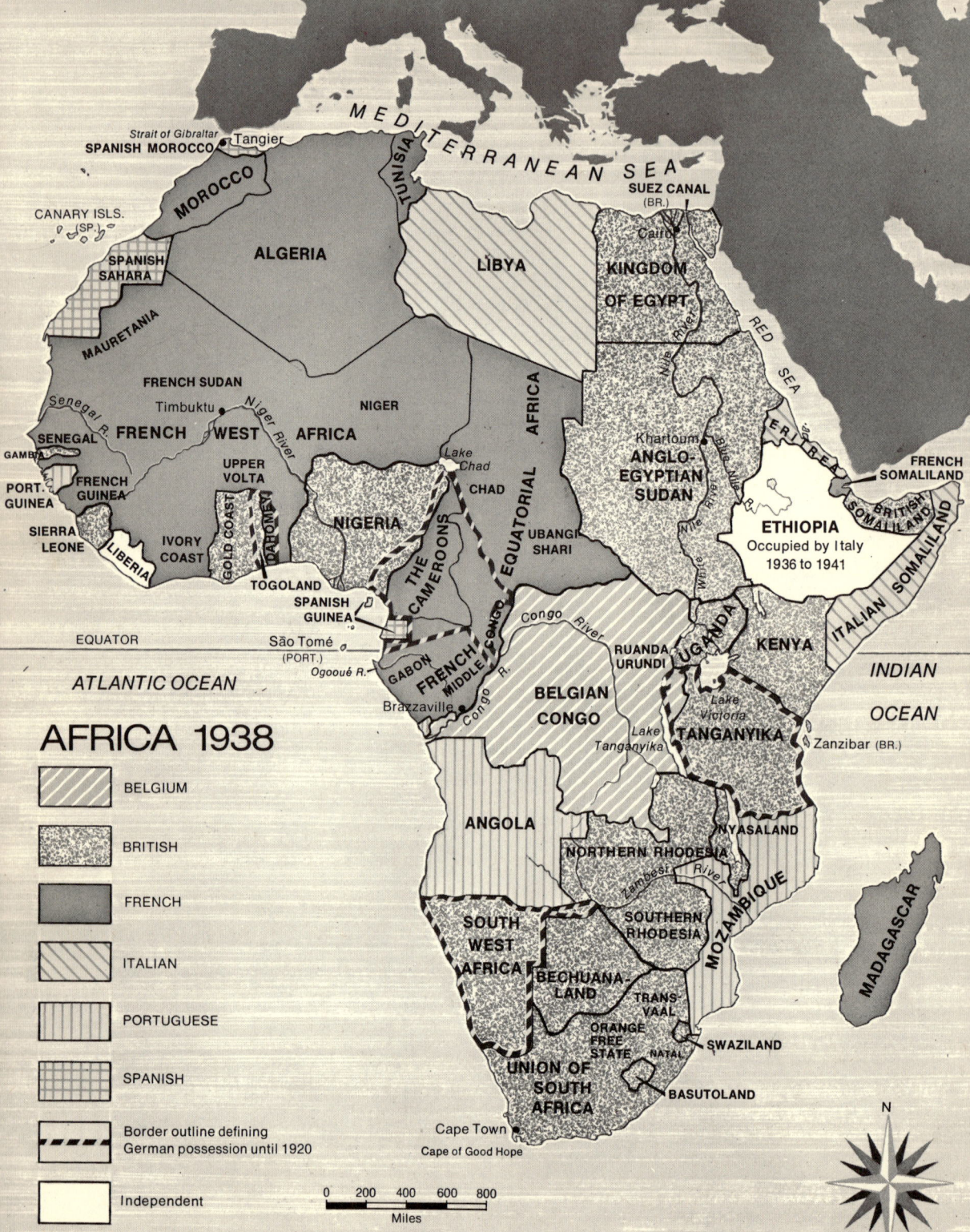

AFRICA 1938

MEDITERRANEAN SEA

Strait of Gibraltar
SPANISH MOROCCO
Tangier
CANARY ISLS.
(SP.)
MOROCCO
TUNISIA
SUEZ CANAL
(BR.)
ALGERIA
LIBYA
Cairo
SPANISH
SAHARA
KINGDOM
OF EGYPT
MAURETANIA
RED SEA
FRENCH SUDAN
Senegal R.
FRENCH WEST AFRICA
Timbuktu
Niger River
NIGER
EQUATORIAL AFRICA
Nile River
Khartoum
ANGLO-EGYPTIAN SUDAN
ERITREA
FRENCH SOMALILAND
SENEGAL
GAMBIA
PORT. GUINEA
FRENCH GUINEA
UPPER VOLTA
DAHOMEY
Lake Chad
CHAD
Blue Nile River
BRITISH SOMALILAND
SIERRA LEONE
IVORY COAST
GOLD COAST
NIGERIA
THE CAMEROONS
UBANGI SHARI
ETHIOPIA
Occupied by Italy
1936 to 1941
ITALIAN SOMALILAND
LIBERIA
TOGOLAND
SPANISH GUINEA
FRENCH CONGO
MIDDLE CONGO
White Nile River
EQUATOR
São Tomé
(PORT.)
Ogooué R.
GABON
Congo R.
Congo River
UGANDA
KENYA
ATLANTIC OCEAN
Brazzaville
RUANDA URUNDI
Lake Victoria
INDIAN OCEAN
BELGIAN CONGO
Lake Tanganyika
TANGANYIKA
Zanzibar (BR.)
ANGOLA
NYASALAND
NORTHERN RHODESIA
MOZAMBIQUE
Zambesi River
SOUTH WEST AFRICA
SOUTHERN RHODESIA
MADAGASCAR
BECHUANALAND
TRANS VAAL
ORANGE FREE STATE
NATAL
SWAZILAND
UNION OF SOUTH AFRICA
BASUTOLAND
Cape Town
Cape of Good Hope

Legend

BELGIUM
BRITISH
FRENCH
ITALIAN
PORTUGUESE
SPANISH
Border outline defining German possession until 1920
Independent

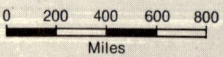

0 200 400 600 800
Miles

N

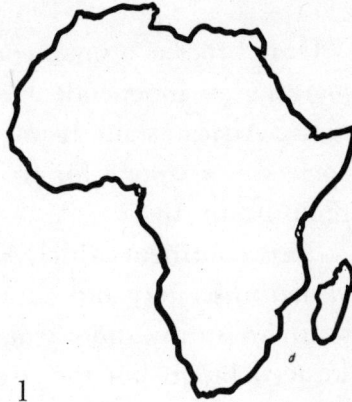

CHAPTER 1

The Stolen Continent

Africa is shaped like a big fat pear, with a great bulge on one side. It is the second largest of the continents, after Asia, with an area of some 11,530,000 square miles, 5,000 miles in length, 4,800 miles wide across the western bulge. Until recently west European governments thought of Africa as being free to take, with each of them having the right to a part. In a period of less than a hundred years they managed to divide up almost all of it.

Take a look at a map of Africa shortly before World War II. More than two-thirds of the continent is shaded in pink and green to represent the colonies of Great Britain and France. The British pink covers over four million square miles; there is almost as much French green. A big chunk of yellow on both sides of the line of the equator marks the Belgian Congo. Italian olive is prominent in the northeast. There are a few strips and dots of Spanish orange in the northwest. Two large purple splotches and a smaller one show Portuguese Africa. Maps made before World War I had substantial areas of German blue, but these have vanished.

3

Only Liberia, a small country on the western coast, is left white, marking an independent African nation. Liberia in fact is not a native African state. It was founded by the American Colonization Society as a colony for freed American slaves and was declared a republic in 1847.

This continent which Europeans found so tempting is widely varied in scenery and climate. The coastal areas of the north and south are sunny and warm, much like southern Europe. Across the western bulge lies the great Sahara Desert, which for centuries could be crossed only with camel caravans. South of the Sahara is the belt of the Sudan, an Arabian word meaning "Land of the Black People," a region of forests and rivers and grazing land. The hot and humid equatorial belt spreads out on each side of the equator. Its deep rain forests are the habitat of Africa's most spectacular animals. Across the equator in the east are towering mountains and mountain lakes. Farther south are more forests and rivers, more deserts, and high barren plateaus, or veld, which slope into the fertile farming region of southern Africa.

Many authorities now believe that Africa was the birthplace of the human race. The East African anthropologist Dr. Louis Leakey has discovered fossils of humanoid or near-human creatures who lived several million years ago. There is evidence of an ancient civilization dating back to 8000 B.C. in the Hoggar Mountains of the Sahara, where magnificent rock paintings have been found. They show wild animals, domestic animals, mythological creatures, and even chariots such as the Egyptians used. The great Egyptian civilization in northern Africa was well established before 3000 B.C.

The Nok civilization in Nigeria, which produced superb terracotta statuary, was flourishing at least by the sixth century B.C. Bronzes of the city of Ife and of the Benin dynasty in the same

*A Benin bronze figure of a
horn-blower, made in Nigeria
about the end of the sixteenth century.
(Courtesy of the Museum of
Primitive Art, New York)*

region rate with the world's finest art. The massive stone ruins of Zimbabwe in Rhodesia mystified white people for years. They refused to believe that Africans had the skill for such work. It is now accepted beyond doubt that the temples and walls of Zimbabwe were the product of African stonemasons. Powerful African kingdoms existed until recent times. Their governments and codes of justice often compared more than favorably with their European contemporaries.

In tropical Africa, early explorers found simple palm-shaded villages laid out symmetrically with wide streets and rectangular mud houses strikingly decorated by geometric designs. Africans early mastered the art of forging weapons and tools. They made elaborate bracelets and anklets of brass or copper, incised with intricate designs. Pottery and basketmaking and leatherwork were ancient and highly developed arts. African masks and statuettes would inspire Europe's Impressionist artists because of their economy of line and rhythmic conception. Africans made their own musical instruments and used the tom-tom to transmit messages over long distances. Their humor is reflected in their folktales about animals. They had their own religions and many believed in a single God. Sharing what they had with their family, clan, or tribal unit was taken for granted, as it still is.

There is great diversity among Africans in languages, customs, ethnic groups, features, and color of skin. Europeans, to justify a policy of aggression, classed them all alike as savages, in dire need of Christian civilization.

The partition of Africa by Europe took place mostly between 1870 and 1900 in such haste it was called a scramble. Because of jealousy and political rivalries, each European power scrambled to get its slice of Africa before someone else could seize it. The methods they used to achieve their aims will be described later. In some places they got lands rich in gold, diamonds, and other minerals. Elsewhere they ended up with arid deserts. What counted in the scramble was not so much the ultimate profits — though fortunes were made through their acquisitions — as the status of having a colonial empire.

In 1884, when the scramble was already well under way, a conference was held in Berlin, attended by representatives of fourteen countries — the European powers and the United States. An act was drawn up whereby all the powers with a "sphere of influence" in Africa were bound to watch over the "moral and material well-being" of the "native tribes." This noble-sounding clause cloaked the real aim of the conference, which was to set up the ground rules for the take-over. Thus it was agreed that any power that annexed new coastal territory in Africa should notify the other powers it had done so. The same ruling was later applied to land in the interior.

In the next years, European nations made treaty after treaty with each other to establish their African claims. Outright warfare between Europeans was avoided, except in the special case of the Dutch and the British in South Africa. There was, however, considerable bitterness and hostility among the weaker nations when they saw the stronger ones grab the prizes.

Neither at the Berlin Conference nor in the treaties that followed it did anyone voice the suggestion that perhaps it was wrong to take Africa from the Africans.

CHAPTER 2

The Earliest Invaders

The ancient world was trading with North Africa when western Europe was still in a state of feudal barbarism. Seafaring Phoenicians from Asia Minor established colonies along the North African coast, of which the most famous was Carthage, in what is modern Tunisia, founded in 814 B.C. Carthage became a Phoenician military base. From it they launched attacks on Sicily, on Sardinia, and finally on Rome. Phoenician traders also ventured down the west coast of Africa, and in 600 B.C., according to the Greek historian Herodotus, they sailed around the entire continent, on the order of the Egyptian pharaoh Necho. The feat took three years.

A Greek colony settled at Cyrene, in eastern Libya, in 631 B.C. Their leader was called Battus. It is said that Battus had gone to the Delphic oracle to ask for a cure for his stammer, but that the oracle had advised him to found a city in Libya "where sheep would find good pasture." According to legend, soon after Battus reached Libya he met a lion and cried out so loudly he never stammered again.

Cyrene, on a hill above the blue Mediterranean, became a Greek city of temples and columns. The Libyans welcomed the strangers at first and gave them their daughters as wives. More Greek settlers arrived. They spread out over the province of Cyrenaica, pushing the Libyans from their own land. When the Libyans called on an Egyptian army to help drive the invaders back, the Greeks defeated the Egyptians. The Libyans continued to wage guerrilla war on them and with the aid of the Carthaginians kept the Greeks from expanding west to the province of Tripolitania.

Alexander the Great of Greece with an army of 40,000 Macedonian soldiers conquered Egypt in 332 B.C. He founded the city of Alexandria, which soon outgrew Carthage and became one of the great cultural centers of the ancient world. Alexander's empire, of which Egypt was only a part, collapsed after his death in 323 B.C.

The Romans invaded Egypt in 58 B.C. The alluring Queen Cleopatra won over Emperor Julius Caesar and Mark Antony, but her charms failed with Caesar's successor, Emperor Augustus, who annexed Egypt firmly to Rome. It remained part of the Roman Empire until A.D. 640.

In 146 B.C., the Romans defeated the Carthaginians and destroyed Carthage. They proceeded to take over all of North Africa from Libya to Morocco. Their occupation was efficient and orderly. They rebuilt Carthage and Cyrene, built Roman cities at Leptis Magna and Sabratha in Tripolitania, and constructed reservoirs and aqueducts to preserve and distribute the limited water supply. They planted olive and fig trees, grew wheat, and raised grapes for wine. In the first centuries A.D., Christianity spread, in spite of the attempts of the Roman rulers to suppress it. Many Christian martyrs were torn to pieces by wild animals in mass spectacles.

The native Berbers, a light-skinned, fiercely independent peo-

Roman invaders entering an Egyptian city.

ple, were recruited into the Roman armies and forced to work on Roman farms and as laborers. Many Berbers fled south to the desert where they lived a free, nomadic existence. When Roman civilization began to decline, the Berbers made frequent raids on their settlements.

In A.D. 429, the Romans were driven out of North Africa by the Vandals, a Baltic people. Their rule lasted a hundred years, and then they were forced out by the Byzantines from the east. In A.D. 640, Arabs from Arabia crossed the Isthmus of Suez into Africa, in the name of their prophet Mohammed, founder of the religion of Islam.

The Moslem Arabs conquered Egypt and founded the city of Cairo, crossed North Africa to Tangier on the Strait of Gibraltar in Morocco, and opened up trade routes across the Sahara to Lake Chad and Timbuktu. They spread south into the eastern Sudan and down the fertile valleys of the Niger River in the west.

The success of the Arabian conquest, which has astounded historians, was largely due to the fact that theirs was a religious conquest. The Moslems judged men not by their wealth nor the color of their skin, but simply as believers or infidels. The Berbers resisted stoutly at first but came to accept the religion of Islam and became Moslems themselves. In A.D. 711, Moslem Arabs and Berbers invaded Spain and remained there for seven centuries; the Spaniards called them Moors. Black Africans also accepted this new religion. In the next centuries Moslem Africans, or those of mixed Arabian-African blood, led conquests of their own and amassed great empires.

The Arabian warriors could be cruel and ruthless, but they paved the way for a high civilization. In the twelfth and thirteenth centuries, Moslem North Africa and Egypt were far in advance of

Europe in mathematics, medicine, and science. Moslem rulers encouraged poetry and kept hundreds of poets in their courts. They built fine cities with libraries and hospitals and mosques.

Corruption in high places and the rise of diverse Moslem sects eventually caused internal dissension, leading to crime and lawlessness. North Africa became known as the Barbary Coast, the land of barbarians. Beginning in the fourteenth century, Barbary pirates ruled the Mediterranean, raided European ships, took loot, and made slaves of their Christian prisoners.

The Ottoman Empire, based in modern Turkey, conquered North Africa in the sixteenth century. The Turkish rulers were notorious for their indifference to the native population. Barbary pirates continued their raids into the nineteenth century. In the Tripolitan War, from 1801 to 1805, the United States sent punitive expeditions against Tripoli. These attacks marked the first step toward ending the power of the pirates.

From the beginning of the Christian era, Arabians had been trading along the east coast of Africa. Regularly Arabian dhows carried gold, ivory, and African slaves to Persia, India, and even China, in return for cargoes of silks, rugs, spices, and other goods. The Islamic religion, which spread easily down the coast, helped to strengthen their position.

Beginning in the tenth century, a series of city-states grew up on coastal islands and east-coast harbors — Malindi, Mombasa, Kilwa, Sofala, Zanzibar, among others. Within their walls rose palaces and private dwellings several stories high. Inside they were furnished with oriental splendor. The wealth of the city-states came largely from the exorbitant import and export taxes they demanded from the ships sailing back and forth across the Indian Ocean. Their ruling class was Arabian and Swahili, the latter a people of mixed

Arabian-African blood. Collectively, the city-states were known as the Zenj Empire.

In this period before the building of the Suez Canal, Europeans had no water route to East Africa. The very existence of the city-states was unknown to them until late in the fifteenth century.

Ships of the Barbary Coast pirates, with their slaves at the oars. (The Bettmann Archive)

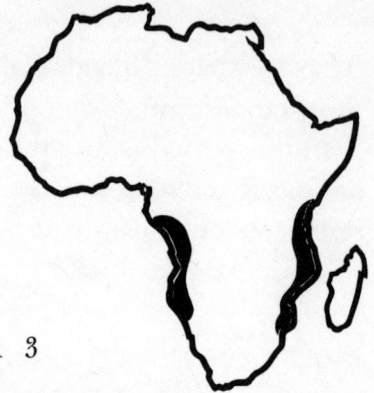

CHAPTER 3

Portugal—Brave Navigators and Ruthless Conquerors

Portugal was one of the smaller and poorer European powers, but it had daring navigators. Beginning in the 1400's, they were sailing down the West African coast, establishing trading posts all along the way. By 1471 they had occupied the island of São Tomé, in the Gulf of Guinea, near the equator.

There was a widespread belief that the waters south of the equator were boiling and filled with sea monsters, but Diogo Cão ventured into them in 1482. He was under orders from the king of Portugal to sail around the continent and find a water route to India. Though he did not get that far, he did discover the Congo, Africa's second longest river after the Nile. On his second voyage, Diogo sailed up the Congo nearly a hundred miles when he was stopped by rapids. On his third, he paid his respects to the king of the Congo at his palace on the hills south of the river.

The kingdom of the Congo was large and prosperous. They had royal roads along which couriers carried messages from the king to the chiefs of his provinces. They used cowrie shells for money.

There was a court of law which punished criminals not by prison or death, as in Portugal, but by giving them as slaves to those they had injured. The slaves were used as domestic servants. Missionaries have reported that the slaves were not ill-treated.

Portugal was soon sending gifts of rugs, furniture, and religious objects to the king of the Congo, who in return filled their ships with copper, ivory, and a few slaves. Under the influence of Portuguese missionaries, the royal family became Christians. Merchants arrived to buy more slaves from local chieftains in return for guns and liquor. The king of the Congo wrote to the king of Portugal that his country was being robbed of its youth. His protests went unheeded. More and more slaves were rounded up, some to work on the coffee and cacao plantations of São Tomé, many more to be shipped to the Portuguese colony of Brazil.

These raids were the beginning of a massive slave trade in West Africa, in which England, France, Spain, Holland, Prussia, Denmark, Sweden, and the United States all took part, and which was in effect a prelude to the later take-over of the continent. In the more than two hundred years the slave trade lasted, an estimated 15 million Africans were transported to foreign lands, principally the Americas and the West Indies, to live out their lives in servitude. Perhaps 30 to 40 million others died before they reached their destination. The total is thought to exceed all the slaves taken by the Arabians in the East in a period of over two thousand years.

Unscrupulous African chieftains cooperated with European and American sea captains by bringing slaves from the interior, where they purposely fomented tribal wars in order to capture the victims. The whole fabric of African society disintegrated as a result. England, which had more slave ships than any other country, was the first to prohibit slavery and the slave trade and took the lead

15

Slave traders loading their ships on the African coast.

in persuading other nations to do so. In the early decades of the nineteenth century, it had almost stopped.

The kingdom of the Congo suffered the most devastation the most quickly from the slave trade. *Pombeiros* — of mixed Portuguese and African blood — went far into the interior to get slaves. Once flourishing villages became empty ruins. In 1665, the Portuguese killed the last of the Congo kings, because he refused to confirm gold and mining concessions granted by his predecessor.

The Portuguese founded the coastal city of Luanda in 1575. It is said that every white settler there had at least fifty slaves; the wealthy owned up to three thousand. In piecemeal fashion they took over all the land of the kingdom of the Congo south of the Lower Congo River. This became the Portuguese colony of Angola, which finally encompassed 481,500 square miles.

In 1498, the Portuguese navigator Vasco da Gama achieved what Diogo Cão had failed to do. He sailed around the Cape of Good Hope, up the east coast of Africa, and on to India, the first European to make this long journey. En route, da Gama saw the dazzling city-states of the Zenj Empire. Although at first the people were friendly, he and his successors systematically destroyed these city-states: plundered their wealth, set them on fire, and killed or enslaved their populations. Today all that is left of their former splendor are a few of their handsome carved wooden doors.

For a time the Portuguese took over the Zenj trade to the Far East, but they lacked the ships and crews to run it efficiently and later lost out to the Dutch and English. Arabians from Oman, in Arabia, ousted the Portuguese from the northern city-states, ruling the area from the island of Zanzibar. Only in the Zambezi River valley in the south could the Portuguese retain power. To get control of the gold trade from the Zimbabwe region, they set up inland

Fort Jesus, on the coast at Mombasa, near Zanzibar, built by the Portuguese in the early seventeenth century.

plantations, equipping the owners with slaves and soldiers of their own. These plantations were the basis of their claim to Mozambique, which became a Portuguese colony of 297,730 square miles. Long after the slave trade was abolished in the West, the Portuguese were shipping slaves from Mozambique to Brazil, via the Cape of Good Hope. Understandably, they never won the affection of the people.

On the basis of early explorations, Portugal tried to claim the inland area between Mozambique and Angola, but the English annexed this territory for themselves.

The other European powers also maneuvered the Portuguese out of their early trading settlements on the west coast, one after another. The Portuguese were able to establish the small colony of Portuguese Guinea — 13,948 square miles — between French Senegal and French Guinea, because England did not want the French to have it. The native inhabitants of Portuguese Guinea remained hostile to the colonists. Portugal established domination only after a series of bloody wars. As late as 1915, colonists were living behind walls in their coastal capital of Bissau, afraid to venture out. The Portuguese rule by force was never accepted.

UNION OF
SOUTH AFRICA

DUTCH

CHAPTER 4

The Dutch and British in South Africa

The Dutch East India Company was formed in 1602 to send fleets of ships to the Far East, along the route which Vasco da Gama had pioneered. On the interminable voyages sailors lived on a diet of hard biscuit and rancid pork. Nearly all fell sick with scurvy and many died. To reduce their losses, the company decided to found a midway station in southern Africa. In 1652, they landed two hundred company employees at Table Bay, west of the Cape of Good Hope, for the purpose of providing their ships with fresh meat, fruits, vegetables, and medicinal herbs. To do the actual farming and hard labor, slaves were brought in from Madagascar, India, and Ceylon, along with a cargo of Angolese, mostly children, from a Portuguese slave ship which the Dutch had captured.

The only native inhabitants on this southern tip of Africa were tiny Bushmen, who lived by hunting with bows and poisoned arows, and Hottentots, who grazed cattle. The Bushmen fled to the hills when the white men came. The Hottentots stayed on, but showed reluctance to work for the Dutch or to barter their cattle.

20

The representatives of the Dutch East India Company landing at Table Bay, South Africa, were met by the Hottentot inhabitants.

In 1653, they killed a young Dutch herdsman whom they found on land they considered their own. This incident led to raids and counter-raids. The settlers with their guns usually won. They took more land as they needed it, pressured the Hottentots into domestic service, and presently added them to their other slaves.

Cape Colony, as they called their settlement, prospered. The settlers built a village, the present Cape Town, with a fortress castle and charming white Dutch-style houses decorated with oriental motifs by their Malaysian craftsmen. Fruit trees and vegetables flourished in the fertile soil. More settlers arrived, including some French Huguenots, who planted grapes for wine. The rich lived well. Some adventurous young men moved far inland and started their own farms, in defiance of company regulations. They became known as Boers, the Dutch word for farmers.

The Boers had a hard, grueling, and dangerous life those first years. They kept their guns in readiness against attacks by wild animals. They lived in mud huts and ate the same food as their Hottentot slaves, whom they nonetheless treated with contempt. As they interpreted their Bible, God had created nonwhite peoples to serve the white race. For sport they went up into the hills and shot down Bushmen as if they were animals.

In time their farms thrived. They built stone houses and raised families. But they kept their narrow-minded ways and were suspicious alike of the comfort-loving people in Cape Town and of missionaries who treated the natives kindly. On a fishing expedition along the Great Fish River, near the east coast, they saw their first black Africans: tall, well-built Xhosa warriors who carried spears. Unlike the timid Bushmen and the docile Hottentots, the Xhosas were afraid of nothing, not even guns, and they far outnumbered the Boers. Throughout the eighteenth century, the Boers and the

Xhosas clashed repeatedly, but their skirmishes usually ended in a standoff.

The Dutch East India Company went bankrupt in 1795. By an arrangement between Great Britain and Holland, the British took over Cape Colony in 1806. The Boers resented British rule bitterly. Their grievances came to a climax in 1833 when the British officially abolished slavery in all their colonies. Between 1835 and 1837 about 10,000 of the stubborn Boers took off with their families, their ox wagons, their guns, and their household goods and headed north. They were called the *Voortrekkers*. Today, a large and rather ugly monument to them stands in the South African city of Pretoria.

The Boer trekkers lived on freshly killed animals or jerked meat. Disease killed their cattle. Water was scarce. They regarded all Africans as their enemy and the Africans soon learned they could expect no mercy from them. According to the missionary David Livingstone, who lived with the Africans and loved them, the Boers in battle sent their Hottentot slaves ahead to serve as shields, and when they took prisoners they killed the men but kept the children as slaves.

Piet Retief, one of the Boer leaders, tried to talk terms with the powerful Zulu king, Dingane, but Dingane suspected treachery and moreover was offended by Retief's bad manners. He ordered the massacre of Piet Retief and all his men. Reinforcements were brought up. On December 16, 1838, the Boers defeated the Zulus at the Battle of Blood River, an event still recorded in South African history books.

The Boers first wanted to settle down in the fertile province of Natal, along the Indian Ocean, but in 1845 the British annexed Natal as their own colony. Still unwilling to live under the British,

Cecil Rhodes.
This was Rhodes's favorite
photograph of himself.

the Boers moved to the high veld of central South Africa, where they established two republics, Orange Free State and the Transvaal. The British did not want this arid land, and they left the Boers alone.

Diamonds were discovered in Orange Free State in 1866. A young Englishman named Cecil Rhodes hurried there, bought up all the mining concessions, and made an immense fortune. Gold was found in the Transvaal in 1884. Europeans, mostly British, flocked to the region to try their luck. The Boers disliked the outsiders and refused them citizenship. Cecil Rhodes, now prime minister of Cape Colony, authorized a raid against the Transvaal under Captain Leander Jameson. The raid failed and Rhodes was forced to resign as prime minister. But disputes between the Boers and the British continued, leading to the Boer War in 1899.

A meeting between the king of the Zulus and a group of Boers in Natal in 1824.

The Boers won the first victories, but the British brought in reinforcements from England and defeated the Boers in 1902. The Union of South Africa, made up of the Transvaal, Orange Free State, Natal, and Cape Province (the original Cape Colony), became a British colony. By the lenient terms of the peace treaty, the colony was self-governing. Except for nonwhites—a term which included not only Africans but descendants of the former slaves—South Africans were allowed to vote and elect their own government officials. Since the Dutch, who became known as Afrikaners, were in the majority, they elected an Afrikaner prime minister. Neither the English settlers nor the home government in London had any noticeable say in how the country was run.

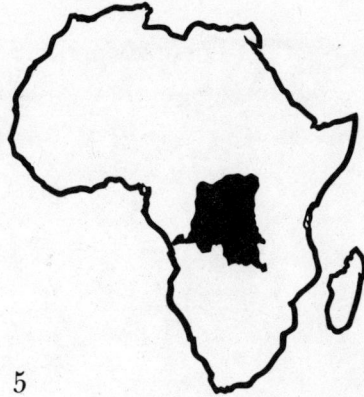

CHAPTER 5

King Leopold and the Belgian Congo

For nearly four centuries after Diogo Cão discovered the mouth of the Congo, the course of this mighty river remained a mystery. The rapids which had kept Diogo from sailing up the river stopped other explorers as well. The mystery of its origin was solved by the Welsh-born journalist Henry Morton Stanley, who grew up in the United States.

With 356 native porters and tons of supplies, including a 40-foot boat built in sections so it could be carried, Stanley set out from Zanzibar, crossed to mainland Africa, and traveled west to a north-erly-flowing river called the Lualaba. Unknown to anyone, the Lualaba was the upper part of the Congo. Stanley followed it for more than a thousand miles to the falls of the Lower Congo, which he descended in part by lowering canoes by ropes and in part by skirting around the surrounding cliffs. On August 9, 1877, he reached Boma, an old slave port near the mouth of the Congo.

The journey took 999 days and cost the lives of 173 members of Stanley's expedition. He was the first white man to see the people

Henry Stanley exploring the islands of Stanley Pool in the Congo River.

who lived along the riverbanks. A firm believer in the supremacy of the white race, he looked on the Africans scornfully and once expressed horror that he and they belonged to the same human race. A shrewd businessman, he observed that the Congo region was rich in minerals, timber, palm oil, and fiber for making rope and paper. Back in England, he tried to interest the British government in exploiting this wealth, but no one would listen to him.

King Leopold II of Belgium heard of Stanley's exploits and summoned him to his palace at Brussels. For years Leopold had been scheming to take his own slice of Africa without offending the larger powers. He decided that the Congo was just what he wanted. He gave Stanley the job of building a road around the rapids of the Lower Congo and of persuading local chieftains to sign over their lands, and the services of their people. Rival nations were led to believe that Leopold's only aim was to set up medical and scientific stations in the interior.

Using native labor, it took Stanley two years to cut a road through the stony cliffs beside the tumultuous river. In December, 1881, he reached Stanley Pool, where the Congo becomes wide and smooth and slow-moving. To his anger, the French flag was already waving on the northern bank of the pool; France was claiming the northern Congo Basin.

Frustrated, Stanley had to be content with dealing with chieftains along the southern riverbanks. He collected dozens of treaties from them. One chief put his "X" on a treaty in return for a piece of cloth each month. To another, who held out a little longer, Stanley granted a red coat with gold facing, 20 red handkerchiefs, 40 red cotton caps, and 128 bottles of Dutch gin. Since none of them could read, it is obvious they had no idea what they were signing away.

In 1885, King Leopold assumed the title of king of the Congo

A European negotiating with an African chief.

Free State, not in the name of Belgium but in his own name. Treaties established the boundary lines with Portuguese Angola to the south and the French Congo to the north. Leopold sent troops to subdue the big African kingdom of Katanga, under the strong-minded king M'Siri. Katanga, rich in gold and diamonds, fell after M'Siri was fatally shot by a Belgian officer. Belgian soldiers, financed by the European Anti-Slavery Society, drove out

30

Arabian slave traders in the east. Leopold received the credit for the victory, which had in fact strengthened his own position and cost him nothing.

To make the Congo a paying proposition, Leopold parceled out land to private companies, giving them rights on rubber and ivory in return for a large share of their profits. The companies built outposts along the Congo and its tributaries, staffed by white agents and an armed African guard. The agents' pay depended on the amount of ivory and rubber they could get the native people to collect. They were authorized to use force when needed.

If local villagers failed to meet their quota, the agents sent out their African guard to punish them. The soldiers, who were recruited from other regions, were instructed to burn the villages and kill the offenders. It was not uncommon for the agents to demand that their soldiers cut off a foot from the corpses as proof they had obeyed orders. Many Africans fled to the jungle, where they often died of exposure and starvation or from attacks by wild animals.

A few missionaries wrote to King Leopold about the atrocities. When he did nothing, they told their terrible stories to the European press. A British consul traveled up the Congo in 1904 and returned with photographs and eyewitness accounts of incredible brutalities. Leopold was finally forced to launch an official inquiry. After a long investigation, the abuses were confirmed. In 1908, the Belgian parliament took over the Congo Free State from their king, renaming it the Belgian Congo. With an area of over 905,000 square miles, the Belgian Congo was more than seventy-seven times the size of its mother country, Belgium.

Estimates of the number of Congolese people who died under King Leopold's twenty-three-year rule run from three to eight million. The king's own profits were admittedly fabulous.

CHAPTER 6

The British North and South

England was the richest of the European powers and the most advanced industrially and economically. In the eighteenth and nineteenth centuries this small country carved out a world empire, over which it was literally true that the sun never set. In Africa, having early established themselves at Cape Colony, the English proceeded at an astounding rate to appropriate the best land in the north, south, east, and west.

Even before British soldiers started fighting the Boers over South Africa, England was expanding her influence in southern Africa, in large part due to the efforts of the diamond magnate Cecil Rhodes, who dreamed of a British Empire stretching "from the Cape to Cairo." As prime minister of Cape Colony, Rhodes disliked the Boers and schemed to keep as much land as possible out of their control.

On the urging of Rhodes, England made a protectorate of Bechuanaland in 1884, an area of 220,000 square miles of grassland and desert, north of the Transvaal. Some of the Bechuana

32

Africans examining a British explorer's boat tied up on the Zambezi River in Northern Rhodesia.

people protested the take-over. They were rounded up and auctioned off in Cape Town as five-year indentured servants. The people of Basutoland, an area of 11,716 square miles set like a mountainous island within South Africa, actually asked England for protection against the Zulus and the *Voortrekkers*. The British annexed Basutoland in 1868 and placed it under Cape Colony, but in 1884 transferred it to direct rule from London as a protectorate. In 1894, the British made Swaziland part of South Africa, but changed its status to that of a British protectorate in 1903, right after the Boer War. This mountainous little country of 6,700 square miles was considered a special prize because of its gold, tin, and asbestos. The Dutch in South Africa strongly resented England's direct rule of these three protectorates—Basutoland, Bechuanaland, and Swaziland.

The British South Africa Company, directed and financed by Cecil Rhodes, brought two more southern African colonies into the British fold: copper-rich Southern Rhodesia (150,333 square miles) and Northern Rhodesia (290,323 square miles). "Rhodes ate up countries for his breakfast," one native king said bitterly.

The conquest began by an agreement between the British South Africa Company and King Lobengula of Matabeleland (in Southern Rhodesia), wherein Lobengula allowed mineral surveys in return for a grant of 10,000 rifles and 100 pounds a month. By 1893, Lobengula had decided that the gifts were a trick to make serfs of his people; he returned the rifles and rejected his monthly fee. Seeing bribery fail, Rhodes turned to force against this "insolent black king." In a decisive battle, more than a thousand Matabele people were killed.

King Lobengula died soon after this defeat. In England there were some outcries about "the Matabeleland Scandal." One anonymous writer called Lobengula a great African hero, comparable to the heroes of ancient Sparta.

The British South Africa Company, unaffected by the protests, imposed its rule on both Rhodesias. They were governed in the name of the company until 1923, when England declared Northern Rhodesia a protectorate and made Southern Rhodesia a self-governing British colony, with the same status as South Africa.

Nyasaland, a strip of 33,686 square miles bordering Northern Rhodesia on the east, was made a British protectorate in 1891. British soldiers fought Arabian slave traders in the region of Lake

34

A Matabele warrior being shot down by a British trooper.

Nyasa until 1896, when the last Arab fort was razed. Cotton, tobacco, and coffee proved profitable crops in Nyasaland. Africans were paid $1.25 to $1.50 a month to farm these crops. It is a moot question whether they were much better off than under slavery.

With the above acquisitions, England controlled, directly or indirectly, all of southern Africa except Portuguese Angola and Mozambique.

In the north, British interest was concentrated on Egypt, which since the building of the Suez Canal in 1869 had great strategic importance. The canal was constructed under the supervision of Ferdinand de Lesseps, who was French, but England acquired financial control of it in 1875 by buying up the Egyptian shares.

Like other Turkish rulers in North Africa, Ismail Pasha, khedive of Egypt, borrowed money right and left, in part for admirable public works such as an opera house in Cairo, in part to satisfy his own extravagant tastes. In 1880, when Ismail's debts to European bankers had mounted to 60 million pounds, the Turkish government replaced him with his son Tewfik Pasha. Tewfik's willingness to do the bidding of the European powers caused a popular revolt under an Egyptian nationalist, Arabi Pasha. The worried British sent a fleet to patrol the Alexandria harbor.

A riot broke out in that city on June 11, 1882, in which several hundred were killed, including fifty Europeans. The police restored order, but Tewfik fled to Cairo, leaving Arabi Pasha in control. On July 11, British ships opened fire on Alexandria. Thousands were killed there. British marines landed two days later to find the city in flames. Certain British statesmen denounced the bombardment as "unnecessarily intense."

British occupation of Egypt was complete by 1884, but the Turks were left in nominal control to "maintain law and order."

Not until 1914 did Egypt officially become a British protectorate. Although Egypt was promised independence in 1923, the last British soldiers did not leave until after World War II.

The eastern Sudan, south of Egypt, a huge territory of nearly a million square miles, had been, in theory, under Egyptian-Turkish control since 1820. But the Egyptian garrisons were hundreds of miles apart, and outside of the principal city of Khartoum on the Nile, powerful slave traders made their own rules. A fanatic Moslem known as the Mahdi organized the Sudanese in a campaign to drive out the "Turks"—their name for all Europeans and Egyptians as well.

The first British foray into the Sudan, in 1883, was a disaster. Under the British chief of staff, Colonel William Hicks, a force of about eight thousand soldiers, mostly Egyptian prisoners of war who had fought with Arabi Pasha, were nearly annihilated by the Mahdi and his followers. The British, discouraged, sent General Charles George Gordon, an old Sudan hand, to Khartoum to arrange withdrawal of the Egyptian garrisons. The Mahdists besieged Khartoum and captured it before reinforcements could be brought in. Gordon was stabbed on the steps of his palace; his severed head was displayed in triumph.

The British stayed out of the Sudan until fifteen years after the Mahdi's death. General Lord Kitchener brought a force of 8,200 British and 17,600 Egyptians up the Nile in a journey that took two years. In 1898, they fought the Mahdists, led by the late Mahdi's best general, Mahmoud, at Omdurman, across the Nile from Khartoum. The Mahdists suffered 20,000 casualties, against British-Egyptian losses of 500. General Mahmoud, a proud and handsome young man, was displayed at the head of a victory parade, with chains riveted on his ankles, a halter around his neck, and his

37

hands tied behind his back. Camp followers of Kitchener's army pelted him with garbage.

In 1899, the Anglo-Egyptian Sudan was proclaimed an Egyptian province. It was made clear that all Egyptian laws in the province must have British approval, and that in all other matters, the British would have the final say.

General Gordon was killed by the Mahdists on the steps of his palace at Khartoum. (Charles Phelps Cushing)

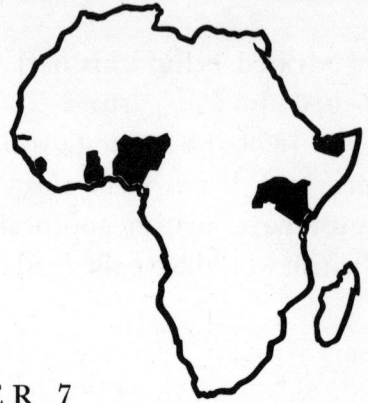

CHAPTER 7

The British East and West

The island of Zanzibar, off modern Tanzania, became the trade center of East Africa after the Portuguese were pushed back to Mozambique. In the 1870's, Sultan Barghash of Zanzibar was the undisputed ruler of the east coast and inland to undefined boundaries from Somaliland to Mozambique. Though the sultan had declared in 1845 that the export of slaves was strictly forbidden, the slave trade still flourished. The slave traders were going farther and farther inland for their victims, whom they sold in the Zanzibar market to local purchasers, often for illegal export. Some of the slave traders grew immensely wealthy and kept palaces and slaves and harems of their own on Zanzibar.

John Kirk, acting British consul on Zanzibar, liked Sultan Barghash personally but never stopped urging him to halt the entire slave trade. Under threat of a British blockade, Barghash reluctantly agreed to do so in 1873. In return, Kirk promised to use his influence to preserve the independence of Barghash's eastern empire. In spite of their agreement, slaves continued to be sold in

40

A slave dhow is driven onto the coast of Zanzibar.

the open market on Zanzibar. Nor could Kirk keep his bargain for longer than a few years.

In the arbitrary manner of the European powers, Germany and England agreed in 1886 to limit the sultan's empire to Zanzibar, two smaller islands, and a strip of mainland coast 10 miles deep and 600 miles long. The rest of the mainland claimed by the sultan was divided up between these two European powers.

England took the northern area. The British East Africa Company, a commercial organization like Cecil Rhodes's British South Africa Company, was given the task of "developing" the country, meaning to take over control.

During 1887, company agents persuaded twenty-one African chiefs to sign treaties granting the British the right to protect them. The British government took charge officially in 1895. Eventually they carved out a colony of 219,730 square miles. First called British East Africa, it was renamed Kenya in 1920. Although Kenya was centered on the equator, much of it was high and mountainous. British settlers found the climate pleasing and profitably grew coffee, sisal, grain, and cotton.

Zanzibar yielded to British protection in 1890. It was henceforth administered under the joint rule of the sultan and a British resident.

Also in 1890 another British-German treaty gave England the right to Uganda, a land of 80,371 square miles between Kenya and the Belgian Congo, bordered by Lake Albert and Lake Victoria. The first white person to visit Uganda's three African kingdoms was the explorer John Speke, discoverer of Lake Victoria. He found certain customs barbarous but was impressed by the advanced social, political, and legal system and the high degree of sophistication of the kings in this isolated region. The kings were friendly to him, as they were later to the traders, the Catholic and Protestant missionaries, and the Moslems who followed. Too late they learned that all these visitors were to be followed by soldiers with guns. In 1894, the Union Jack was hoisted over Uganda and it became a British protectorate.

In 1884, Great Britain acquired one more territory in East Africa, a roughly triangular strip of land of 68,000 square miles between the Gulf of Aden and Ethiopia, which became British Somaliland. The Somalis were a pastoral people who had already lived under Arab rule and Egyptian rule and were staunch Moslems. When the British took over, the Somalis organized under

Sayyid Mohammed ibn-Abdullah. British soldiers called him the Mad Mullah. He and his followers launched guerrilla attacks until his death in 1920. Sayyid Mohammed is now regarded as the "Father of Somali nationalism." Even without his harassment, the hot dry climate made British Somaliland a wretched place for the British stationed there.

British marines and sailors attack a stronghold of the mullah in Somaliland in May, 1904. The sketch was made by a British officer.

In West Africa, the British holdings consisted of four colonies all separated from each other by French or German colonies. From north to south they were Gambia, Sierra Leone, Gold Coast, and Nigeria. In the same order they increased in size from Gambia to Nigeria.

England's annexation of Nigeria, an area of over 300,000 square miles, began in the 1840's when, to help police the slave trade, she seized two Portuguese settlements, one at Lagos, Nigeria's capital, and the other on the many-pronged estuary of the Niger, Africa's third largest river.

African coastal chieftains, who had been making large profits by bringing slaves from the interior, resented and obstructed the British presence. Among these was King Kosoko of Lagos, who finally ceded his state to the British for a pension of one thousand pounds a year. Another was a former slave named Jaja who had become a powerful merchant-king. Jaja agreed to sign a treaty with the British in return for their promise to protect him from the French. He was exiled to the West Indies where he died.

Sir George Goldie of the Royal Niger Company was granted a British charter to trade up the Niger for palm oil and other products. Goldie undercut his French competitors, made treaties with some African rulers, but resorted to machine guns to conquer the Moslem-African kingdom of Nupe. The British government took over his operations in 1899 and proclaimed Nigeria a colony and protectorate. Within its arbitrary boundaries were the Yorubas, the Ibos in the southeast, the Hausas in the north, and other African tribes whose own claims to sovereignty would henceforth be ignored.

The Gold Coast (modern Ghana) received its name because of alluvial gold deposits which had successively attracted Portugal,

Denmark, and Sweden. The British declared the coastal area a colony in 1874. Their inland occupation was opposed by the independent and warlike Ashanti nation. In 1896, a large British expedition captured the Ashanti capital of Kumasi and exiled the king, the queen mother, and other Ashanti officials to the Seychelles islands in the Indian Ocean.

Sir Frederick Hodgson, governor of the colony, went to Kumasi in 1900. He made a grave error by ordering the Ashantis to turn over to him their golden stool, so he could sit on it. He thought the stool was their king's throne, but to the Ashantis it represented the soul of their nation. No one ever sat on it; it rested on its side on a stool of its own. To them, Hodgson's demand was sacrilege. They besieged him in Kumasi for two months before he could get reinforcements. Ashanti and the Northern Territories (the area north of the Ashanti kingdom) were officially declared British protectorates and part of the Gold Coast Colony in 1901.

The British referred to the Gold Coast, an area of 92,100 square miles, as their "African jewel," because of its rich gold mines and fertile soil.

Sierra Leone was the name the Portuguese gave a mountainous peninsula extending into the Atlantic. In 1791, the British granted a charter for the area to a philanthropic organization, St. George's Bay Company. They called it Freetown (the present capital of Sierra Leone) and turned it into a settlement for liberated slaves, some from America, who had fought with the British in the American Revolution, others from Canada, England, Jamaica, and central and southeast Africa.

The explorer and writer Sir Richard Burton visited Sierra Leone in 1863 and was amazed to see former slaves sitting on juries and taking part in local government. Many of them had even as slaves become more European in their ways than African. For years the largely Moslem native inhabitants regarded them as intruders.

The peninsula of Freetown became a crown colony in 1808, but not until 1895 was inland Sierra Leone, about 28,000 square miles, taken under British protection. Three years later the British imposed a hut tax and there was a general revolt, put down by force. After 1906, diamond mining turned Sierra Leone into a profitable investment.

Gambia had the distinction of being Africa's smallest colony, a narrow enclave of 4,000 square miles set in Senegal, extending along both banks of the Gambia River. Following the Portuguese, the British established a settlement at Bathurst, at the mouth of the Gambia, in 1588. The French ousted them in 1817, but in 1891 agreed to let them have the land to the limit of the Gambia's navigability.

CHAPTER 8

The French Overseas Territories

Unlike her rival European powers, France had a liberal tradition, born in the slogan of the French Revolution, "Liberty, Equality, Fraternity." The French spoke of their African colonies as "Overseas Territories" and in theory regarded all the Africans living in them as equals, entitled to French citizenship. But like the other powers, the French did not ask the African people whether they wanted to be ruled by France. They preferred making treaties with the African kings or governors or chieftains. When that did not work, they used force.

The French overseas territories were grouped mainly in French North Africa, French West Africa, and French Equatorial Africa. Algeria, Tunisia, and Morocco made up French North Africa. The Arabians said of the inhabitants of these three countries: "The Algerian is a man, the Tunisian is a woman, the Moroccan, a lion."

Algeria, a figurative stone's throw across the Mediterranean, tempted France because of its fertile semitropical coastal area and its unexploited mineral resources. In 1827, the French consul went

47

to see the Turkish dey, or governor, of Algiers, about some unpaid wheat payments. The dey, who detested Europeans, got angry and struck him with a fan. France promptly set up a naval blockade around Algiers. In 1830, three years later, they landed 37,000 French infantry, cavalry, and artillery.

The native Berbers refused to come to the dey's support. Within three weeks, he surrendered. Christian rule did not appeal to the Berbers either. They revolted under their leader, Abd-el-Kader.

The dey of Algiers struck the French consul during an interview in 1827, precipitating a French blockade of Algiers.

A contemporary French popular print depicting the seizure of Algiers by French forces in 1830.

The French used such brutal tactics to subdue them that Abd-el-Kader agreed to exile to save his people from ruin. Instead he received a long-term prison sentence. He was later freed by Napoleon III. Though uprisings continued for a score of years, by 1848 France felt secure enough to declare Algeria — an area of 920,000 square miles — a French territory.

French settlers were encouraged to come and live in Algeria. They fell in love with the country, the brilliant flowers and lush foliage, the picturesque Moslem cities, the vast desert dotted with oases where date palms grew. In time, French Algerians thought of Algeria as home, which would cause complications when native Algerians asked for independence.

In 1881, the French landed troops in Tunisia on the excuse that Tunisian outlaws had crossed into Algeria. The Turkish bey of Tunis, whose people were on the verge of revolt because of the shameless way he and his ministers had been robbing them, promptly placed himself under French protection. There were some uprisings against French occupation in the countryside but within a year order was restored. In 1883, Tunisia was declared a French protectorate.

The Turkish sultan of Morocco practically delivered his country to Europe by demanding large loans which he spent on automobiles, bicycles, pianos, cameras, and even dolls and a zoo. In 1906, twelve European nations and the United States agreed to place the country under international control, leaving France to handle the policing of it. France declared it a protectorate two years later, leaving Spain a few small coastal areas, buying off the other powers by concessions elsewhere. Tangier, on the Strait of Gibraltar opposite Spain, became an international port. The sultan was allowed to keep his title but his power was limited to religious matters. Violent uprisings by Berbers in the Riff Mountains, under Abd-el-Krim, continued until 1927.

French West Africa included most of Africa's western bulge, most of the northern shore of the Gulf of Guinea, all of the Sahara not part of North Africa, and extended inland across more than half of the continent. It totaled 1,841,200 square miles. After much changing of names and boundaries France divided it into eight colonies: Mauretania, Senegal, Guinea, the Ivory Coast, and Dahomey, all bordering the Atlantic Ocean or the Gulf of Guinea; and French Sudan (now Mali), Upper Volta, and Niger, all inland.

France began this mammoth conquest at the mouth of the Senegal River, where they had established a trading settlement in 1637. General Louis Faidherbe, who became governor of Senegal in 1854, united several isolated coastal trading posts, established a port at Dakar, Senegal's present capital, fought off Moslem tribesmen who tried to raid the settlements, and built a fort to withstand El Hadj Omar, king of the Fulani people. Fulani warriors opposed the French until 1883, when Captain Joseph Gallieni signed a treaty with King Ahmadu, son of El Hadj Omar, placing his lands under French protection.

A more formidable foe was Samori Touré, whose empire covered much of inland Senegal, Ivory Coast, Guinea, and the Sudan. With the aid of Senegalese soldiers, France cut into his empire a little at a time. Guinea was made a protectorate in 1849. France also en-

A group of charging Riff cavalrymen in Morocco in 1925. (United Press International Photo)

listed, willingly or not, the people they "liberated" from Samori. France controlled most of Senegal in 1893, although Samori Touré refused French protection for the remains of his empire until 1898, when he no longer had a choice. Ivory Coast became a French protectorate in 1893.

King Behanzin of Dahomey on the Gulf of Guinea also gave strenuous opposition to the French, with the aid of his Amazons, a dauntless army of women. Dahomey became a French colony in 1894 and the French promptly disbanded the Amazons.

The conquest of the French Sudan, Niger, and Upper Volta was long and slow. The ancient African kingdoms of Ghana, Mali, and Songhai that had once ruled these lands were supplanted by powerful Moslem empires, with armies equipped with guns, and shrewd and sophisticated leaders who could not be bought off by a few trinkets and cases of rum. Though a French force captured Timbuktu, the center of Sahara caravan trade and a former Moslem cultural center, in 1893, the rest of the French Sudan was not effectively occupied until 1914. Niger, farther west, became a colony in 1921; the Upper Volta, in 1919. The French Sudan and Niger each occupied nearly a half million square miles, and the Upper Volta, over 100,000 square miles. Outside of colonial circles, they remained virtually unknown until all three became independent nations and members of the United Nations.

Mauretania on the Atlantic, another area of over half a million square miles, is sparsely populated and mostly desert. Although European powers recognized the French "sphere of influence" in Mauretania in 1817, France did not bother to declare it a protectorate until 1903 and did not officially make it a colony until 1920.

French Equatorial Africa totaled some 960,000 square miles, extended from French West Africa south to the Belgian Congo, and included Gabon and the Middle or French Congo on the coast and two landlocked colonies, Chad and Ubangi-Shari (now the Central African Republic).

The French "influence" in Equatorial Africa began with their settlement at a former slave port on the mouth of the Ogooué River, in Gabon. Here they founded Libreville in 1849, as a home for slaves who had been freed or escaped their masters. In 1874, when Stanley was launching his spectacular voyage down the Congo, an Italian-born French naval officer, Savorgnan de Brazza, was taking a small expedition up the Ogooué. About 400 miles from the coast, at modern Franceville, he left the Ogooué and marched south on foot almost to the Congo. He made friends with the native peoples on the way, learned their languages, and studied their customs.

On Brazza's return to Europe, King Leopold of Belgium invited him to join Stanley, whom he had just hired to build his Congo empire. Brazza refused coldly and instead persuaded the French to sponsor another expedition aimed at keeping the northern Congo basin out of Leopold's clutches. Again Brazza traveled up the Ogooué and cut south, reaching the smooth and placid waters of the Middle Congo while Stanley was still building a road around the rapids of the Lower Congo. King Motoko of the Bateke people, impressed because Brazza came not as a warrior but as a man of peace, signed a treaty with him, placing all his kingdom north of the Congo under French protection.

Brazza raised the French flag on the north bank of the Congo at Stanley Pool. The site would later become Brazzaville. It was this French flag which so enraged Stanley when he arrived months later. He never forgave Brazza for getting there first. Boundaries between Leopold's Congo Free State and the French Congo were not settled until 1894.

King Motoko arranging a treaty with Savorgnan de Brazza placing his kingdom north of the Congo under French protection.

Brazza continued his explorations, between Brazzaville and the coast and far inland up the Ubangi, a major Congo tributary. Everywhere he talked to the Africans about the benefits of French protection. Other French explorers established French claims to Ubangi-Shari, an area of 247,700 square miles, and Chad, 495,600 square miles, west of Niger.

The French wanted to extend their rule through the eastern Sudan — abandoned by the British after their 1883 defeat by the Mahdists — and on to the Nile Valley and the Red Sea. In 1896, Captain Jean Marchand with 7 French officers and 120 Senegalese riflemen set out from the Atlantic and marched some 2,600 miles across Africa. The group suffered hunger and hardships and Marchand nearly died of fever. Ragged and emaciated, they reached Fashoda (modern Kodok), some 400 miles south of Khartoum, in

54

July, 1898. They were still entrenched there two months later when the British general Kitchener with his massive army defeated the Mahdists at Omdurman.

General Kitchener joined Marchand at Fashoda. Though the captain proudly indicated he was ready to fight until death for France's claim to the eastern Sudan, Kitchener sensibly proposed that they have a drink and let their home governments thrash the matter out. France later conceded that the Anglo-Egyptian Sudan was in the British sphere of influence.

In East Africa, France managed to get only one small property, French Somaliland, 9,073 square miles, at the juncture of the Gulf of Aden and the Red Sea. Without interference from the other powers, she did annex the island of Madagascar across the Mozambique Channel, an area of 227,678 square miles, in 1896, and the smaller Comoro Islands.

France allowed African representatives from their territories to sit in the French parliament long before other European powers considered such a step. Such representation was in fact limited, and injustices existed in French Africa as they did elsewhere. When Savorgnan de Brazza paid a return visit to the French Congo in 1905, he discovered with horror that the natives to whom he had promised French protection were being exploited in the cruelest manner, to gather rubber, ivory, palm oil, and to work in the copper mines. Heartbroken and bitter, he died the same year.

CHAPTER 9

Germany Joins the Race

Germany came late to the African scramble. Before 1871 there was no German nation, only a federation of German states. Following the Franco-Prussian War of 1870, during which Premier Bismarck of Prussia led the other German states to victory over the French, the German Empire was created, with Bismarck as chancellor. Bismarck at first opposed taking colonies. He was overruled by the German parliament, by powerful shipping firms already doing extensive trade in East and West Africa, and by religious groups who felt that their government should give protection to German missionaries in Africa.

In 1883, a German manufacturer, F. A. E. Lüderitz, signed a treaty with an African chieftain which gave Lüderitz a piece of land 215 miles square at the Bay of Angra Pequena, on the southwest coast. Bismarck asked England if they had any claims over that region. When there was no immediate reply, Bismarck declared the Angra Pequena settlement under German protection. This was the nucleus of German South-West Africa, a territory of some

318,000 square miles of desert and grazing land and then-unknown mineral resources in copper, tin, gold, and diamonds.

German administration began in 1892. The native Hereros and Nambibians opposed their new rulers but were shot down without mercy. At least half of the Nambibian population and an estimated 65,000 of the some 80,000 Hereros died those first years. The survivors were left homeless and had the choice of fleeing to the desert or working for the Germans, who gave them near-starvation wages and flogged or even murdered them for the slightest disobedience. The brutality of the German administrators in South-West Africa became as notorious as that of King Leopold's agents in the Congo.

In July, 1884, the German Foreign Office sent their consul at Tunis, Dr. Gustav Nachtigal, to the Cameroons and Togoland on the Gulf of Guinea, allegedly to make a scientific survey. Within a few weeks Dr. Nachtigal had made treaties with local rulers and raised the German flag on the coast of both countries. The British had tentative claims on the area, but their protests came too late.

The Cameroons, betwen British Nigeria and French Gabon, eventually encompassed 166,489 square miles. Long after German occupation, the native population remained hostile. When commercial agents ventured into the interior after palm oil, groundnuts, ivory, or rubber, they had to travel with an armed military escort. So many settlers died of tropical diseases that the Cameroons became known as the white man's graveyard.

In Togoland, a strip of land about 34,600 square miles lying between British Ghana and French Dahomey, Germany had little trouble. It was the smallest of her colonies and for a long time the only self-supporting one.

German activities in East Africa also began in 1884. In November, a fanatic German nationalist, Dr. Karl Peters, arrived by steerage at Zanzibar with two companions, crossed over to the mainland, and disappeared into the interior. Their purpose, they said, was to study East Africa's flora and fauna, but within a short period Peters had persuaded local chieftains to mark their "X" on treaties granting concessions of 60,000 square miles, all in exchange for gifts of rum and childish trinkets. Chancellor Bismarck had not sponsored Peters, but when Peters returned with the treaties in February, 1885, Emperor Wilhelm I decreed German protection over the area he had signed up.

Sultan Barghash of Zanzibar claimed the same area as part of his empire, but by August, 1885, four German naval vessels were anchored threateningly off Zanzibar and he had no forces to oppose them. As related before, the sultan's friend, the British acting consul, John Kirk, could do nothing. England had no desire to offend Germany at this stage. She and Germany agreed to divide up East Africa for themselves, leaving the sultan a 600-mile coastal strip, which Germany later purchased. German East Africa, subsequently called Tanganyika, became a colony of 360,000 square miles, extending to Lake Tanganyika and the Belgian Congo in the east, Kenya on the north, and Mozambique and Nyasaland in the south.

Dr. Karl Peters, who began it all, was later recalled because his cruelty to the Africans created a scandal. The German rulers were in general so contemptuous of the inhabitants, including the coastal Arabians and Swahilis, that in 1888 there was an insurrection against all Europeans. Germany sent in warships, and the British, alarmed for the safety of Kenya, loaned one thousand Sudanese troops. The uprising was suppressed by their combined forces. The leader, Bushiri, was captured and executed.

The highland climate of Tanganyika, like that of Kenya, was

ideal for European settlers. The Germans applied scientific methods to raising sisal for hemp. It was Germany's largest colony and became the most productive.

When World War I broke out in Europe, the fighting spread over into Africa. Before the end of 1914, Anglo-French forces had captured German Togoland and the Cameroons, and the British had taken Tanganyika. South-West Africa was captured by soldiers from the Union of South Africa.

East Africans marching under the German flag, about 1913.

Algerian cavalrymen escorting German prisoners at the close of World War I. (United Press International Photo)

Africans fought side by side with their oppressors in what was hailed as "the war to make the world safe for democracy." France alone enlisted 680,000 Africans, many of them the stalwart Senegalese. There is no doubt that the fighting caused more death and destruction in Africa than all of the African tribal wars of the past.

By the terms of the Treaty of Versailles, Germany was shorn of her African colonies. In 1920, the League of Nations parceled them out to the Allies in the form of mandates, with the proviso that they were to promote the welfare of the inhabitants and protect them from "slavery, militarism, liquor, and drugs." The possibility of returning the land to the Africans was never considered.

France received most of the Cameroons and more than half of Togoland, which she retained under the same names. England received the western strip of the Cameroons, which was integrated with Nigeria, and western Togoland, which became part of the Gold Coast. Belgium was granted a mandate over Ruanda and Urundi, two small provinces of Tanganyika bordering the Belgian Congo. England was given a mandate over the rest of Tanganyika; thus the dream of Cecil Rhodes of a British African Empire reaching "from the Cape to Cairo" was at last fulfilled. The Union of South Africa was granted direct control over South-West Africa.

Italy, which had fought with the Allies, received nothing at all.

The distribution of the German colonies later proved grist to the propaganda mill of Adolf Hitler. In 1939, just before his take-over of most of western Europe, he declared that amends must be made for their theft. Hitler's plan of world domination included a totally German Africa.

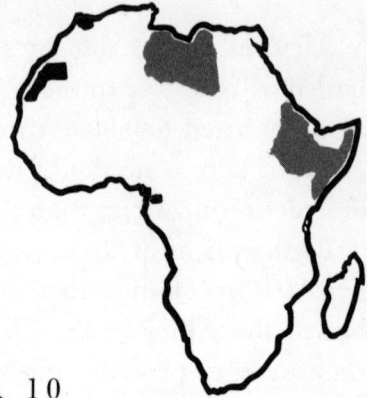

SPAIN

ITALY

CHAPTER 10

Spain and Italy—Stepchildren of the Partition

When the Spaniards drove out the Moors who had ruled them for seven hundred years, they pursued them across the Mediterranean and occupied a number of North African ports. For a time Spain alternated with the Turks in dominating the Barbary Coast. In 1560, Moorish pirates massacred 18,000 Spaniards on the island of Jerba, off modern Tunis, and built their skulls into a great tower. The Spanish were forced to withdraw all their forces except those in coastal Morocco.

The period of the late sixteenth and seventeenth centuries was the age of Spain's glory. Spanish literature and art flourished. Spanish *conquistadores* placed the gold of the Incas and the Aztecs at their king's disposal. He spent it recklessly on European wars. At its height the Spanish Empire included most of South America and the West Indies, part of North America, and the Philippines. By the time the African scramble got under way, Spain was in a decline. Stripped of most of her American colonies, unsuccessful in Europe, she was reduced to a third-rate power.

Guerrilla chiefs in a Riff encampment in Morocco in 1925. (United Press International Photo)

When France took over Morocco, she left Spain a few strongholds, a strip 200 miles long and 60 miles wide in the Mediterranean, including the fortress towns of Ceuta and Melilla, and another tract on the Atlantic, surrounding the town of Ifni. In all, Spanish Morocco covered 28,000 square miles. The Spanish, like the French in Morocco, were for years under attack by Abd-el-Krim and his Berbers from the Riff Mountains. Abd-el-Krim, who had been educated at the Moslem university at Fez, had received his training in the Spanish Moroccan army. For a long time, the large number of Spanish killed in the Riff Rebellion was kept a secret in Spain. It was the French who finally put down the rebellion in 1927.

Río Muni, between Gabon and the Cameroons, on the Gulf of Guinea, had once been a Spanish slave-trading port. In 1875, the other European powers agreed to let Spain keep Río Muni, along with the island of Fernando Poo and several smaller islands. These holdings became Spanish Guinea, a colony of 10,785 square miles.

Spain's largest African possession was Spanish Sahara, an area of 105,448 square miles, bordering Morocco on the north and Mauretania on the east and south, and composed of two zones, Río de Oro and Saguiet el Hamra. When the Spanish raised their flag there in 1889, no other European power protested their occupation of this sparsely settled desert wasteland.

Of all the European colonies in Africa, those of Spain were the least profitable, the most costly to maintain, and totaled the smallest area.

Italy, like Germany, was not a united nation when the scramble began. The different Italian states were united about 1870, under Victor Emmanuel II. They were behind the other powers in industrialization and lacked administrators capable of organizing a colonial empire.

Many Italians left their poor and overpopulated country to settle in North Africa. Italian bankers were among the first to loan money to the extravagant Turks who ruled North Africa in the name of the Ottoman Empire. Yet they had to sit by and watch England take over Egypt, and France absorb Algeria, Tunisia, and Morocco. It was said of the Italians that they had "to pick up the crumbs that fell from the rich man's table."

Neither France nor England claimed Libya, an area of nearly 700,000 miles but the least desirable part of the Mediterranean coast. In 1911, when the Turkish ruler objected to Italian commercial activities in Tripoli, Italy declared war. In this short war, Turkey backed down and let Italy move into Libya. The Italians were driven out in World War I by Bedouins armed by Germany and Turkey, but they returned in 1922. The province of Tripolitania was considered pacified the next year. The people of Cyrenaica resisted Italian occupation until 1932. Even afterward, it cost Italy large sums to police this troublesome colony.

Italian explorers pointed out to their government that though the British and French had occupied northern Somaliland, they had ignored the southern part, an area of about 193,000 square miles extending along the Indian Ocean to Kenya. By 1889, the entire area had been taken under Italian protection. Two years later, Captain Filonardi, Italian consul at Zanzibar, formed a company to govern and develop the land. Filonardi's company failed. Its successor, the Benadire Company, was unable to function because of an insurrection of the Somali people. The Italian government took formal control of the area in 1906 and gave Italian Somaliland the status of a colony.

Eritrea, an area of 48,350 square miles, was a desert coastal strip along the Red Sea, separated from the ancient kingdom of Ethiopia by a rugged plateau and mountain range. The Italian Rubattino

65

Shipping Company set up a coaling station on the Eritrea coast in 1869. With British permission, the Italians extended their sphere of influence and made Eritrea an Italian colony in 1890.

Italy hoped to make Eritrea a stepping-stone to Ethiopia, which no other European power had threatened, and made several forays across the border, but the Ethiopians drove the Italians back. When Menelik, negus (king) of Ethiopia, found that Italian agents were trying to bribe the outlying tribal people, he won the tribes' loyalty by quoting an African saying: "Of a black snake's bite you may be cured, but from the bite of a white snake you will never recover."

Menelik also refused to abide by an Italian-sponsored treaty that he had been tricked into signing, which granted him five thousand Remington rifles and a loan of four million lire, in return for his agreement to let Italy handle his dealings with other European powers. "One independent power does not seek the aid of another to carry on its affairs," Menelik said.

A decisive battle took place near Adowa, well within the Ethiopian border, in February, 1896. The Italians had 17,700 troops, of which 40 percent were Africans. Menelik's army had some 90,000 troops. Italian casualties mounted to 6,000 dead, 1,500 wounded, and 2,000 taken prisoners. The Ethiopians mutilated at least 800 of their prisoners, mostly by amputation of the right hand and left foot. By the peace settlement, Italy agreed to stay within the former borders of Eritrea.

Italians brooded over the defeat at Adowa for almost half a century. "Avenge Adowa!" became a rallying cry of fascist dictator Mussolini. On October 2, 1935, Italian motorized troops crossed the Ethiopian border in three places. Adowa was captured quickly. Ethiopians, armed mostly with ancient muskets or curved sabers, fought bravely but could not halt the advance. Appeals by Emperor

66

King Menelik of Ethiopia discussing a peace treaty with Italian commissioners. (The Bettmann Archive)

Haile Selassie mounting the steps of the Royal Residence in Addis Ababa, after his reentry into the city in May, 1941. (United Press International Photo)

Haile Selassie to the League of Nations proved futile, as did his attempt to purchase arms and ammunition in Europe.

On December 6, Italian planes dropped bombs on the city of Dessie, history's first mass air raid on civilians. More planes dropped mustard gas, which inflicted horrible burns on the barefoot Ethiopian warriors. On May 5, 1936, the Italians marched into Addis Ababa, capital of Ethiopia. The long-independent country became an Italian colony.

The Italian occupation lasted exactly five years. During this brief period Italy occupied over 1,274,000 square miles in Africa, about one-ninth of the continent and considerably more than "crumbs . . . from the rich man's table." In the early part of World War II, the British helped Haile Selassie form his guerrilla warriors into an army of liberation. The Ethiopian emperor made a state entry into Addis Ababa on May 5, 1941.

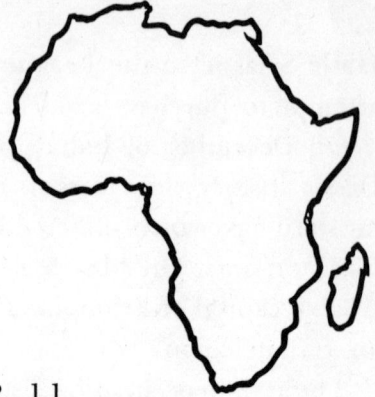

CHAPTER 11

The Continent Is Returned

Some enormous changes took place in Africa under colonial rule. Once-small coastal and river trading settlements became large modern cities with fine harbors, skyscrapers, hotels, shops, and palatial mansions or pretty villas for the white residents. Here and there factories and timber mills and mines scarred the landscapes. Some of the mining companies became industrial empires controlled by international bankers and foreign stockholders. European-run farms extended over thousands of acres.

Railroads and highways opened up once-impenetrable jungles. Steamers supplemented African pirogues along the navigable rivers. With the advent of the airplane, flying became the preferred method of travel for those who could afford it. From impressive airports built near the major cities, transcontinental planes took the colonists home to Europe in a matter of hours. Small bush planes carried them easily across the wilderness through which their hardy predecessors had painfully struggled for months or years.

Kenya, Nairobi, in 1950 (top) and 1913 (bottom). (United Press International Photo)

Africa's wild animals, slaughtered recklessly by "white hunters" and deprived of their normal hunting and grazing grounds, diminished at an appalling rate. More than half a million lions, elephants, buffalo, antelope, and zebras were shot down under orders of the colonial government of Southern Rhodesia, on the mistaken theory that the massacre would get rid of the tsetse fly, which carries the microorganism causing sleeping sickness in domestic cattle and humans. The white rhinoceros, among other rare animals, came near to extinction.

Under pressure from nature lovers as far away as the United States, some colonial governments set aside huge areas as national parks, where visitors could photograph animals but were not permitted to harm them. Some people claim that these animal sanctuaries were Europe's greatest contribution to Africa.

The Europeans did not attempt to industrialize the whole continent. Off the highways and away from the cities, the landscape remained unchanged. In remote villages people lived much as their forefathers had done, built their huts of mud and thatch, held their ancient ceremonial dances, communicated with neighboring villages by means of their talking drums. But increasingly the rural villages were left in the hands of women and children and the aged, as the young and able-bodied men flocked to the cities.

The whole structure of colonial society depended on a large supply of cheap labor. Africans in large numbers went to work for the white men, not always unwillingly. They took jobs in the mines and in the factories, on farms, as household servants and waiters — all the menial work. The excitement of the white man's world had an appeal for them. They acquired a taste for things Europeans took for granted: automobiles, radios, solidly built houses, watches, and cameras, which for the Africans were all luxuries they could rarely afford. Their own superb arts and handicrafts were replaced by wares to please white tourists, including ashtrays, bookends, and salad bowls.

Even when the worst abuses of forced labor were halted, Africans received a fraction of the pay of white workers. Their employers took the attitude that this arrangement was necessary and inevitable. If Africans went on strike for better pay, the police were called in to force them back to work. There were instances when strikers were shot down.

Many Africans adopted Christianity, and their enthusiasm and devotion remained undampened by the fact that not all white people practiced the Christian precepts their missionaries taught. A few Africans started their own Christian sects with large followings. In the Belgian Congo, the colonial administration imprisoned the leaders of two such purely African Christian movements; they feared they were teaching the people to revolt. To a greater degree than most Europeans realized, Africans retained the religion of their ancestors and saw no inconsistency in mingling Christian ceremonies with their own.

Beginning with the missionaries, Europeans provided schools for African youth. In primary grades the children learned to speak and read and write in the languages of their conquerors. A genuine hunger for knowledge was aroused, but very few African parents had the means to send their children to private secondary schools. A minute percentage won scholarships to study in European or American universities and returned home as doctors, lawyers, priests or ministers. They became the elite of African society, the people who were largely responsible for organizing the national movements leading to liberation. The education of African girls was notoriously neglected.

Europeans also introduced modern medicine, built large African hospitals, and set up small rural dispensaries. There were never enough hospitals, enough doctors and nurses, to meet the needs of a large population suffering from diseases worsened by poverty, lack of sanitation, and malnutrition.

It was a common thing for Europeans to boast of the benefits of Christian civilization they provided their African subjects. In truth, if there was one constant which they gave them, it was hunger. Hunger was no stranger in Africa in the old pre-colonial days, but never was it so widespread. After the Europeans came, there was hunger in the rural villages where subsistence farming was left to women and old people. There was hunger in the cities, where African workers on small salaries could not properly feed their large families. Hunger existed among the few who held white-collar jobs and felt it a matter of pride to dress themselves and their children in a manner similar to that of their better-paid white colleagues. There was hunger among the educated elite who so craved knowledge that they bought books rather than nourishing food. There was hunger in families where men took to drink to forget their daily frustrations and humiliations. The hunger was not something that people talked of or complained about. If the Europeans took it for granted that Africans preferred mealie porridge to the roasts and broiled chicken on their own tables, the Africans did not enlighten them.

It has been pointed out again and again that while Europe enriched itself from the minerals and the agricultural products of Africa, the African people were deprived of their own heritage and of their dignity as human beings. Still, some African educators say they are grateful to the Europeans, not because of the benefits of their civilization, but because European culture enlarged their

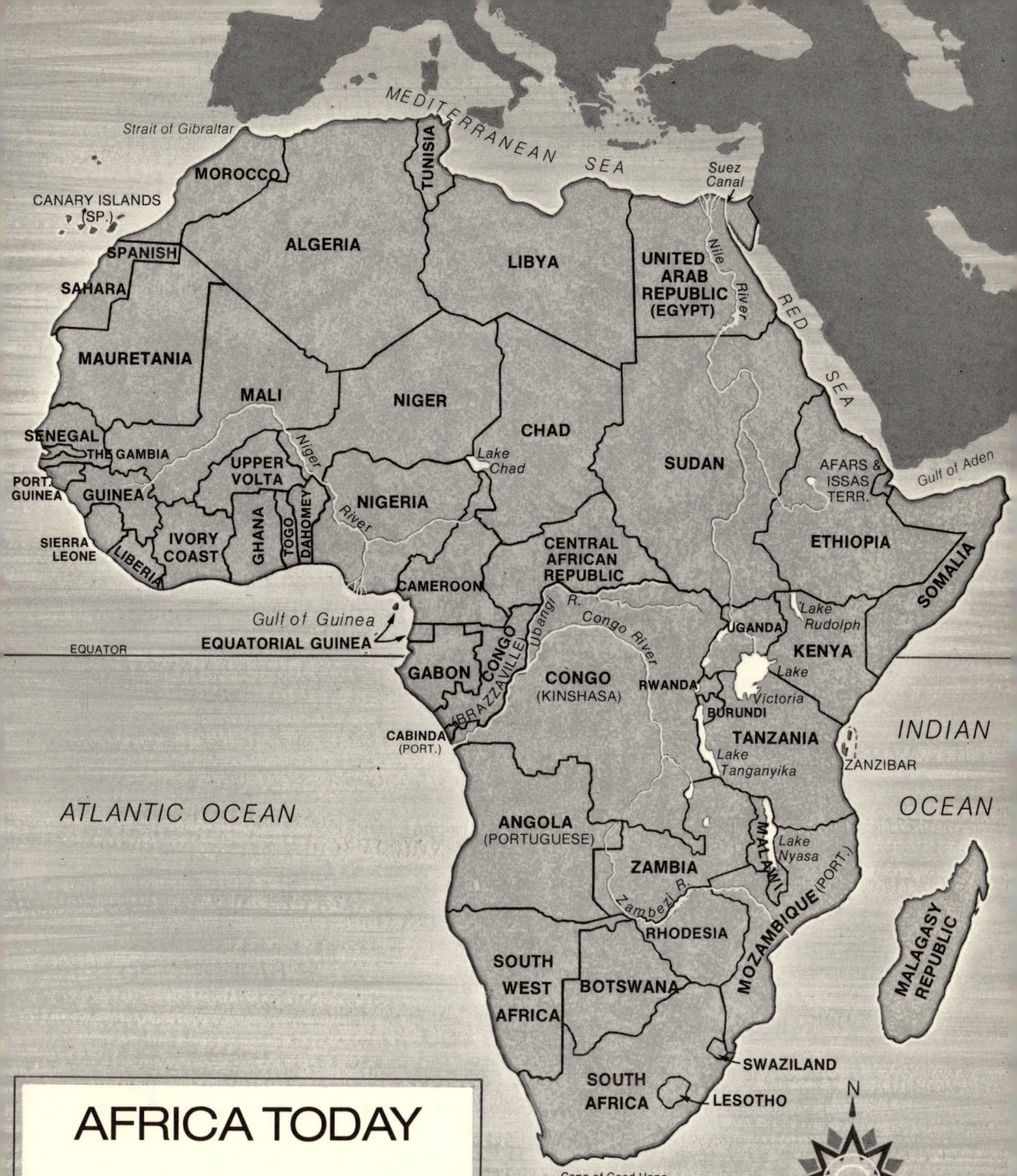

MEDITERRANEAN SEA

Strait of Gibraltar

CANARY ISLANDS (SP.)

MOROCCO

TUNISIA

SPANISH SAHARA

ALGERIA

LIBYA

UNITED ARAB REPUBLIC (EGYPT)

Suez Canal

Nile River

RED SEA

MAURETANIA

MALI

NIGER

CHAD

SUDAN

Gulf of Aden

AFARS & ISSAS TERR.

SENEGAL

THE GAMBIA

PORT. GUINEA

GUINEA

UPPER VOLTA

Niger River

DAHOMEY

NIGERIA

Lake Chad

CENTRAL AFRICAN REPUBLIC

ETHIOPIA

SOMALIA

SIERRA LEONE

LIBERIA

IVORY COAST

GHANA

TOGO

CAMEROON

Ubangi R.

Congo River

UGANDA

Lake Rudolph

Gulf of Guinea

EQUATORIAL GUINEA

EQUATOR

GABON

CONGO (BRAZZAVILLE)

CONGO (KINSHASA)

RWANDA

KENYA

Lake Victoria

BURUNDI

INDIAN

CABINDA (PORT.)

TANZANIA

Lake Tanganyika

ZANZIBAR

OCEAN

ATLANTIC OCEAN

ANGOLA (PORTUGUESE)

MALAWI

Lake Nyasa

MALAGASY REPUBLIC

ZAMBIA

MOZAMBIQUE (PORT.)

Zambezi R.

RHODESIA

SOUTH WEST AFRICA

BOTSWANA

SWAZILAND

SOUTH AFRICA

LESOTHO

Cape of Good Hope

N

AFRICA TODAY

0   200   400   600   800
Miles

horizon, gave them "new vistas, new visions." The Europeans challenged them, however accidentally, to take their rightful place in the world of the future.

The role of European colonists in Africa was totally unlike that of the early European settlers in America, who made a new life for themselves and became Americans. European residents of Africa never thought of themselves as Africans and did not relinquish their European identity. They were there to help govern the colonies, to make money, or for charitable work. Before agreeing to go to Africa, government employees and technicians demanded contracts for limited periods of time and provision of travel expenses to Europe for their annual vacations. The relatively few permanent white residents preferred the delightful climate of South Africa or coastal North Africa or the highlands of Kenya and Tanganyika, and avoided Africa's mysterious and menacing interior.

Some of the saddest effects of colonialism were perhaps on the colonists themselves. Once in Africa, these white people acquired a "colonial mentality." Convinced of their own superiority, they cloistered themselves in their all-white circles, trying to ignore the life surging around them. Bored and dissatisfied, they missed a marvelous opportunity to enrich their own lives by getting to understand people of a different cultural background.

The period of European rule was fairly brief in terms of history in most parts of Africa — rarely more than a hundred years, and less for the most part.

On the modern map of Africa, the French green has now vanished except for the small dot marking Afars and Issas, formerly called French Somaliland. The colonies in French North Africa, French West Africa, and French Equatorial Africa are now all

A vast crowd gathered in a square in Khartoum on August 16, 1955, while the Sudan Parliament was voting in favor of the expulsion of British troops as a step toward national independence. The equestrian statue is one of Lord Kitchener.

independent African nations. The former French Congo is now the Republic of the Congo. Its capital is still called Brazzaville.

Across the river, the Belgian Congo has become the Democratic Republic of the Congo. Leopoldville, its capital, has been renamed Kinshasa, after an African village once on that site. To avoid confusion, the two Congo republics are popularly called Brazzaville Congo and Kinshasa Congo.

There is no longer a trace of British pink on the African map. The former British colonies also are now independent nations. Three of them, however, are still under white rule.

The Republic of South Africa, though freed from its ties with England, is ruled by a white minority government, mostly Afrikaners, the descendants of the Dutch Boers. Under their policy of apartheid, the nonwhite population, especially black Africans, are victimized by discriminatory laws unparalleled in history.

South-West Africa, which was transferred from German rule to British South Africa under a League of Nations mandate, is still under the control of South Africa, in spite of a United Nations resolution that the mandate is no longer valid. Africans in South-West Africa are subjected to apartheid, even more stringently than in South Africa.

Rhodesia, the former Southern Rhodesia, is also ruled by a white minority. Because of its harsh racial policies, all countries but Portugal and South Africa have broken diplomatic relations with Rhodesia.

Some of the new African nations formerly under British rule accepted the status of membership in the British Commonwealth, along with such nations as Canada and Australia. In the same way most of the French colonies agreed to the proposal of the then-president, Charles de Gaulle, to become part of the French Community

President Jomo Kenyatta (right rear) reading a speech at the opening of the Kenya Assembly, December 14, 1964. (United Press International Photo)

of nations. Guinea was one country that refused this proposal, in spite of its obvious trade and commercial advantages. President Sékou Touré of Guinea reportedly told de Gaulle that his people preferred "freedom in poverty to riches in servitude."

Italy too has disappeared from Africa. Libya, which oil discoveries have now made wealthy, was granted independence after World War II. Eritrea is now part of Ethiopia. Italian Somaliland, united with British Somaliland, makes up the Somali Republic, or Somalia.

Spain has lost most of its holdings, but retains the garrison towns of Ceuta and Melilla, as well as Spanish Sahara.

Portugal has clung doggedly to her sizable territories of Mozambique, Angola, and Portuguese Guinea. In all three areas African guerrillas are fighting for independence. In spite of Portuguese bombing raids, some with napalm, these guerrillas have liberated large areas.

No one can guess when Africa will throw off its remaining foreign shackles, but it is generally agreed that outright colonization is old-fashioned, outmoded, and inevitably doomed.

Africa Today — Colonial Background

COUNTRY	MAJOR EUROPEAN INFLUENCE	PRESENT STATUS
Afars and Issas	France colonized (French Somaliland) in 1896	French Overseas Territory since 1967
Algeria	France took control in 1830	Independent since 1962
Angola	Portugal first settled in fifteenth century	Portuguese Overseas Province
Botswana	Britain made protectorate (Bechuanaland) in 1884	Independent since 1966
Burundi	Germany made part of German East Africa in 1895 (Urundi); Belgium occupied in 1916	Independent since 1962
Cameroon	Germany colonized in 1885; France and Britain occupied in World War I	French Cameroon became independent in 1960
Central African Republic	France colonized (Ubangi-Shari) by end of the nineteenth century	Independent since 1960
Chad	France took control in 1900	Independent since 1960
Dahomey	France controlled by 1894	Independent since 1960
Democratic Republic of the Congo (Kinshasa)	Leopold II of Belgium took control in 1885	Independent since 1960
Equatorial Guinea	Spain took over in 1778	Independent since 1968
Ethiopia	Italy occupied 1936–41	Traditionally independent; constitution proclaimed in 1931
Gabon	France took control in 1910	Independent since 1960

81

COUNTRY	MAJOR EUROPEAN INFLUENCE	PRESENT STATUS
Gambia	Britain colonized in 1588	Independent since 1965
Ghana	Britain colonized in 1874 (Gold Coast)	Independent since 1957
Guinea	France established protectorate in 1849	Independent since 1958
Ivory Coast	France controlled by 1893	Independent since 1960
Kenya	Britain controlled by 1895	Independent since 1963
Lesotho	Britain took over in 1868 (Basutoland)	Independent since 1966
Liberia	Colonized by freed slaves from United States in 1822	Independent since 1847
Libya	Italy took control in 1912	Independent since 1951
Malagasy Republic	France took control in 1896 (Madagascar)	Independent since 1958
Malawi	Britain took control in 1891 (Nyasaland)	Independent since 1964
Mali	France controlled by 1914 (French Sudan)	Independent since 1960
Mauretania	France controlled by 1903	Independent since 1960
Morocco	France and Spain shared control by 1912	Independent since 1956
Mozambique	Portugal settled in sixteenth century	Portuguese Overseas Province
Niger	France colonized in 1921	Independent since 1960
Nigeria	Britain entered in 1840's	Independent since 1960
Portuguese Guinea	Portugal controlled by 1886	Portuguese Overseas Province
Republic of the Congo (Brazzaville)	France controlled by 1885	Independent since 1960
Rhodesia	Britain took over in 1893 (Southern Rhodesia)	Independent since 1964
Rwanda	Germany controlled by 1899; Belgium took over after World War I	Independent since 1962
Senegal	France took control by 1893	Independent since 1958
Sierra Leone	Britain took control in 1895	Independent since 1961

COUNTRY	MAJOR EUROPEAN INFLUENCE	PRESENT STATUS
Somalia	Britain controlled (British Somaliland) by 1884; Italy (Italian Somaliland) by 1906	Independent since 1960
South Africa	Dutch settlers arrived in 1652; Britain took control in 1806	Independent since 1934
South-West Africa (Namibia)	Germany controlled by 1892; South Africa took over during World War I	Under *de facto* South African control, disputed by the U.N.
Spanish Sahara	Spain took control in 1889	Spanish Overseas Province
Sudan	Britain and Egypt shared control from 1889	Independent since 1956
Swaziland	Britain established protectorate in 1903	Independent since 1968
Tanzania	Germany took over (German East Africa) in 1886; Britain took control in 1920 (Tanganyika)	Independent state made up of Tanganyika and Zanzibar since 1964
Togo	Germany took control in 1884; France and Britain shared control in 1914	Independent since 1960
Tunisia	France took control in 1881	Independent since 1956
Uganda	Britain took over in 1890	Independent since 1962
United Arab Republic	Britain established protectorate in 1914 (Egypt)	Independent republic since 1953
Upper Volta	France made colony in 1919	Independent since 1960
Zambia	Britain controlled by 1894 (Northern Rhodesia)	Independent since 1964

Index

87

ABOUT THE AUTHOR

Robin McKown was born in Denver, Colorado, and spent her childhood vacations in a ghost mining town called Ward, in the Rocky Mountains. She received a degree from the University of Colorado and also studied both at Northwestern University and the University of Illinois. After her marriage she moved to New York and worked in several different fields, including writing book reviews and radio scripts for the Book-of-the-Month Club.

For the past dozen years, writing books for young people has been her full-time occupation. It has involved considerable travel. From an extended stay in the northern mining region of France came *Janine* (a winner of the 1961 Child Study Association Award) and a boy's story of the French resistance, *Patriot of the Underground*. She has made several trips to Africa and has visited a number of the former colonies discussed in *The Colonial Conquest of Africa*.

At present Mrs. McKown lives on a 97-acre farm made up mostly of wooded hills in western New York State.